# SHIRE NATURE

# THE NIGHTJAR

## PETER TATE

## CONTENTS
The nightjar family 2
Distribution and population 7
Nesting and breeding behaviour 15
Song 20
Food 21
Folklore 22
Useful information 24

Cover: *A nightjar in a typical attitude silhouetted against the sunset.*

Series editor: Jim Flegg.

Copyright © 1989 by Peter Tate. First published 1989.
Number 48 in the Shire Natural History series. ISBN 0 7478 0030 8.
All rights reserved. No part of this publication may be reproduced or transmitted in any form or by any means, electronic or mechanical, including photocopy, recording, or any information storage and retrieval system, without permission in writing from the publishers, Shire Publications Ltd, Cromwell House, Church Street, Princes Risborough, Aylesbury, Bucks HP17 9AJ, UK.
Printed in Great Britain by C. I. Thomas & Sons (Haverfordwest) Ltd, Press Buildings, Merlins Bridge, Haverfordwest, Dyfed.

# The nightjar family

The European nightjar (*Caprimulgus europaeus*) is a member of the family Caprimulgidae which consists of some seventy species split into eighteen genera. Within this family there are two subfamilies, the Caprimulginae (goatsuckers) and the Chordelinae (nighthawks), the latter found only in the New World. Nightjars are widely distributed within the tropics and temperate zones but are absent from New Zealand, many oceanic islands and regions of high latitudes. In general the family are medium sized birds measuring from 16 to 41 cm in length with some species reaching 78 cm. A few species are endowed with greatly elongated wing feathers extending to as much as 70 cm in length, which makes these birds the largest of the nightjars, although much of their length consists of 'streamers'. The basic coloration of the family is subdued and benefits birds which are active only in twilight and at night but need good camouflage during daylight hours when they are incubating their eggs, brooding their young or roosting. Their plumage, although sombrely coloured, is a beautiful and subtle combination of vermiculated browns, greys, buffs and black, with whitish wingbars or tail spots in some species.

## THE EUROPEAN NIGHTJAR

The European nightjar is a medium sized member of the Caprimulginae subfamily with no significant size differences between the sexes. The average weight of the male is 87 grams and that of the female 83 grams. The mean wing length is 192 mm in the male and 195 mm for the female with tail measurements of 137 mm and 136 mm respectively. Juveniles have shorter tails and their wing length is marginally less. This combination of long wings and tail gives the bird a very distinctive silhouette as it wheels and glides in a buoyant, rather erratic, flight when hawking for moths and other insect prey. The overall colour is mottled brown in a vermiculated pattern of buffs, dark brown and pale rufous brown. The male has white spots on the three outer primary feathers and the outer tail feathers have white tips, both of these white areas being very conspicuous in flight. The legs of the nightjar are rather short and the inner edge of the middle toe is serrated, a distinctive feature which it is thought may be used when preening. This comb-like feature is shared with a few other groups of birds including the herons, barn owls and dippers. The female is very similar to the male but lacks the white wingbars and tailspots. The juveniles are difficult to separate in the field from adult females, although they tend to have greyer underparts.

The eyes are very large and physiologically well adapted for locating insects in conditions of extremely low light intensity. The eyes of birds are highly specialised and closely adapted to the particular needs of the species concerned. The principal structural difference in the eye of a diurnal bird compared to a primarily nocturnal one lies in the ratio of two kinds of visual cells forming the surface of the retina, known as 'rods' and 'cones'. The rods are sensitive to a low light intensity whilst the cones provide visual acuity. These basic cell types are present in man and other mammals, but in birds the density of the cells in certain areas of the retina is exceptionally high, for example reaching one million visual cells per square millimetre in the buzzard (*Buteo buteo*), as compared to some 200,000 in man. Nightjars and some other nocturnal birds also possess a number of specialised rod cells which lack a tiny oil droplet. These cells, present in most diurnal birds but not required by a nocturnal one, aid colour recognition. If caught accidentally in a beam of light such as car headlights or a torch, the deep orange glow reflecting from the eyes of the nightjar is very striking.

Nightjars undergo a complete postnuptial moult which commences in July and lasts until September. The extent of the moult varies between individuals at any given time, however, some replacing their body and head feathers before departure whilst others set out on migration still in worn plumage. Moult is suspended during migration and is com-

*1. A male hovering with tail depressed clearly showing the white wing bar and white spots on the outer tail feathers.*

*2. Enlarged drawing of the foot of a nightjar showing the serrated middle claw.*

pleted after the bird reaches its wintering area. A partial moult also occurs during the winter and is completed between late January and March before the northward migration begins.

There is some evidence to show that the European nightjar, when experiencing poor weather conditions and consequent food shortages, achieves some degree of torpidity. A number of birds have been found cold and stiff with their pulses, breathing rates and body temperatures lowered as a result of a severe depletion of body fat reserves and ensuing weight loss. In captive birds this process has been shown to be reversible, but there is so far no positive evidence that this occurs in the wild state. It is known, however, that a normal nightjar has two daily temperature minima which occur around midday and midnight, with a maximum temperature during its more active periods at dawn and dusk. Compared with many other bird species, relatively small numbers of nightjars have been ringed and, since the recovery rate is only around 2.6 per cent, mortality and longevity figures can only be approximate. The oldest known bird found so far was eight years old. An analysis of nightjar recoveries up to the end of 1984 revealed that 75 per cent of deaths, where causes were known, were the result of road accidents.

## RELATED SPECIES

Apart from the European nightjar (*Caprimulgus europaeus*), the only other member of the nightjar family which breeds in Europe is the red-necked nightjar (*Caprimulgus ruficollis*), which is to be found throughout the Iberian peninsula apart from a narrow strip in the north. Its range extends to north Africa from Morocco to Tunisia. Slightly larger than the European nightjar, its coloration is rather browner overall with a more prominent pale area on the throat and a reddish-brown nape from which it derives its name. Its flight is stronger and more direct than that of the European nightjar, but in view of the general difficulties attending nightjar identification it is best separated from its relatives by its call. This is a staccato 'cut-ock cut-ock' repeated ninety to a hundred times a minute, though sometimes this call rate may rise to almost twice that speed. The sound carries a long way and may be clearly heard at distances of up to 400 metres. Like the European nightjar the red-necked nightjar produces 'wing-claps' in order to advertise its territory and also possesses a similar 'co-ic' flight call. Little is known about its migration routes and precise winter quarters except that they lie in west Africa.

A third species of nightjar, the Egyptian nightjar (*Caprimulgus aegyptius*), has occurred in Europe as a very rare vagrant. In appearance it is a much paler bird than the European nightjar and it is slightly smaller. It is primarily a desert bird, a native of the drier flatter regions of north Africa, parts of north-east Saudi Arabia and southern USSR (Kazakhstan). Generally it is to be found in flat open areas of hot desert or semi-desert but it avoids the most arid regions too far from any water as well as wooded and mountainous areas. In western Europe the Egyptian nightjar has been recorded in Sweden, Denmark, West Germany and Italy, but only once in Britain, at Rainworth in Nottinghamshire, where one was shot by a gamekeeper in 1883.

## SUBSPECIES

As might be expected of a bird with such an extensive range, the European nightjar is divided into five generally accepted subspecies. These show a variation in both colour and size from west to east and from north to south. In accordance with general biological rules the birds which breed in the north tend to be larger than those in the more southerly part of their range, while birds from the wetter areas are darker in colour than those inhabiting the drier regions. The entire picture is complicated by the fact that within the nominate race *Caprimulgus europaeus europaeus* there is an appreciable variation in colour and size across its range. The following is a general and simplified description of the other subspecies.

*Caprimulgus europaeus meridionalis* breeds in the Iberian peninsula, southern Europe, the Balkans, Turkey, western Iraq and southern USSR. It is a slightly smaller bird than the nominate form and shows longer white markings on the wings than *Caprimulgus europaeus europaeus*. *Caprimulgus europaeus unwini*, which ranges from eastern Iraq, extending into Tien Shan and parts of Pakistan, is paler and greyer. *Caprimulgus europaeus zarudnyi* from the wooded steppes of Kazakhstan is more or less intermediate in general size and colouring between the nominate form and *unwini*. *Caprimulgus europaeus plumipes* from Sinkiang and parts of Mongolia is pale in colour like *unwini*, but its ground colour is a cinnamon-buff rather than grey. *Caprimulgus europaeus dementievi* from north-east Mongolia and southern Transbaikalia is pale and greyish, its whole plumage being heavily vermiculated together with yellowish underparts.

In general the nightjar family forms a homogeneous group apart from a few species which possess special features connected with their sexual display. Such features occur in the pennant-winged nightjar (*Macrodipteryx vexillaria*), a migratory species of sub-Saharan Africa. During the breeding season, the males of this species develop two greatly elongated ribbon-like wing feathers which in some individuals can reach up to 700 mm in length and trail behind the bird when in flight like pennants from the mast of a ship. Such feathers are only present from December to March, being moulted as soon as the breeding season is over.

3. *Red-necked nightjar incubating.*

4. *Egyptian nightjar* (top left) *at the nest in Iran; the very pale colour blends almost perfectly with the surrounding sand.*

The standard-winged nightjar (*Macrodipteryx longipennis*) of West and Central Africa also has two greatly extended wing feathers but these are of an entirely different shape to those of the previous species. They consist of a long wire-like shaft approximately 450 mm long ending in a broad flat plume which commences some 120 mm from the tip. When in flight they trail above and behind the bird giving the impression of two small birds chasing a large one.

The great majority of nightjar species are to be found in the tropics and sub-tropics and, because they are all almost entirely insectivorous, those nesting in temperate latitudes are forced to migrate to warmer regions during the winter period. Until they discovered that many birds migrated, our forefathers thought that birds such as swallows hibernated in winter along with hedgehogs, bears, bats and many reptiles. Since the nineteenth century, however, virtually no one believed that any birds hibernated, so it came as something of a surprise when it was found that one species of nightjar, the common poorwill (*Phalaenoptilus nuttallii*) from western North America, has been found hibernating, hidden away in cracks in the rocks, and there is evidence to indicate that the bird may return to the same hibernation spot in successive winters. During the long period of dormancy the body temperature drops to between 18 C to 19 C instead of the normal 40 C to 41 C. It is possible that only a small percentage of the total poorwill population may adopt hibernation as an answer to winter cold instead of migration. Some other families of birds, such as the swifts and the humming-birds, also possess this ability to lower their body temperature at night or for short periods when food is scarce, but the poorwill is so far the only species in which hibernation has been proved to occur. Aware that the bird did hibernate, the Hopi indians of North America named it *holchko*, 'the sleeping one'.

The common nighthawk (*Chordeiles minor*) of North America is physically similar to the European nightjar but is a far less crepuscular bird, often seen in daylight hunting its insect prey above roofs and streets in cities as well as in the countryside and woods. Nest sites vary considerably and include gravelly soil, barren rocks, vineyards, cornfields, tarred flat roofs in cities and even in gardens. Exceptionally, a nest has been recorded on a wooden rail fence at a height of 2.5 metres.

An interesting group within the nightjar family are the frogmouths (Podargidae), a family of largish nightjars from the oriental and Australasian regions (except New Zealand). They share with the more traditional nightjars the soft plumage and vermiculated coloration of that family but differ in certain anatomical features. Although along with the rest of the nightjar family they have the wide flattened bill adapted for capturing insects in flight, they adopt a different method of hunting for food. Instead of aerial feeding for moths and other night-flying insects with a slow and wavering flight, the frogmouths obtain much of their food by making sallies from an elevated perch and also by hawking insects amongst the branches of trees. They will also, on occasion, eat small mammals which they encounter. Whereas most nightjars rely on their exceptionally effective camouflage for protection on the ground the frogmouth, by contrast, perches in an upright posture on a tree where, completely motionless with its head held upwards and its bill partly open, it bears a remarkable resemblance to a broken tree stump.

Exhibiting a physical similarity to the frogmouths, the potoos (Nyctibidae), of which there are five species, form another nocturnal and crepuscular group of birds which are all resident in the neotropical region. Like other nightjars they too possess plumage which gives them almost complete invisibility when perched and, like the frogmouths, they disguise themselves as tree stumps during daylight hours. They hunt in a similar manner to that adopted by shrikes, flying out to capture their food from a perch to which they return in order to eat their prey. The potoos differ somewhat from other nightjar species in that some members of the family emit pleasant and melodious calls of a rather haunting quality as well as a variety of less musical cries.

A small family within the sub-order Caprimulgidae is the owlet-nightjar (Aegothelidae), a group which is made up of eight species. Resident in Australia and Papua New Guinea these small (200 - 240 mm) and rather endearing arboreal nightjars have large eyes placed well to the front of their heads, which give them a distinctly owl-like appearance. They possess the same wide and shallow beak as other nightjars, similarly surrounded by very pronounced rictal bristles. Unlike the typical nightjar, however, the owlet-nightjar captures most of its prey, consisting mainly of terrestrial insects, on the ground although they do occasionally catch flying prey. They also differ from the true nightjars in that they make their nests in cavities in trees or, rarely, in holes in a cliff face. Their eggs, three or four in number, are placed on a carpet of green leaves.

Although not a member of the nightjar family in the strictest sense some reference should be made to the oilbird (*Steatornis caripensis*) which is a member of the same order. This remarkable bird lives in deep caves in Trinidad and northern South America and spends most of its life in total darkness. In order to be able to fly and find its nest under such conditions the oilbird has developed a means of echo-location. It emits a series of rapid clicking sounds the responding echoes of which indicate the presence of any objects in its path. This form of obstacle avoidance is well known in bats and, in a rather less well developed form, is also used by some of the swiftlets (Collocalia). The oilbird is unique amongst its family in that it eats fruit, a very unusual characteristic in a nocturnal bird. The principal food is a kind of oily palmfruit to which the bird is attracted by smell, the fruit being plucked from the forest trees by the bird whilst in flight. To assist in such activity the oilbirds have a hooked bill reminiscent of a bird of prey. As a result of the oily food being fed to them the nestlings grow enormously fat and are sometimes collected by the local inhabitants who then boil them down to provide themselves with an edible oil. Although, as far as is known, the oilbird is the only member of the order to employ true echo-location, there is some circumstantial evidence to show that the European nightjar may also use some form of auditory location when taking insects in flight. Whilst a great deal more research and investigation is required before any conclusions can be reached, this remains an interesting possibility.

# Distribution and population

As can be seen from the map, the European nightjar is a summer breeding visitor to much of Europe and Asia, ranging across the whole of the western Palaearctic region as far north as 63 degrees and southwards and eastwards to include much of Turkey, Iran and parts of Soviet Central Asia, Pakistan and possibly Nepal, just reaching China in Sinkiang province. In Africa it is found as a breeding bird in the north-west of the continent in Morocco and Algeria extending as far east as the western parts of Tunisia.

DISTRIBUTION IN THE BRITISH ISLES

The present distribution of the nightjar in the British Isles is mainly concentrated in a number of pockets, almost all of which lie to the south and east of a line from the Humber to the Severn. The main stronghold of the nightjar in southern England is undoubtedly an area comprising the New Forest, the heaths of west Surrey, Sussex and, to a rather lesser extent, the Dorset and east Devon heaths. There is a further centre of population in the Breckland in East Anglia and there are small numbers on the coastal heaths of Suffolk. Outside these areas there are moderate breeding populations on the North Yorkshire moors, Cannock Chase in the west Midlands and a few in Wales. Numbers breeding in Scotland have fallen considerably, particularly in Galloway, although the populations on the Isle of Arran and in Kirkcudbright and Argyll seem to have been maintained fairly well.

5. Owlet-nightjar — an owl-like head on a nightjar body.

6. Standard-winged nightjar showing the extremely elongated wing feathers raised above the bird as it displays.

*7. Male nightjar gliding with wings raised and tail spread.*

In Ireland it is now a rare bird with only two or three pairs being recorded each year.

## POPULATION

Sadly, since it is such a fascinating and graceful bird, the European nightjar has tended not only to contract in range but also to decrease in numbers as a breeding species. This decline, possibly starting at the end of the nineteenth century, has continued throughout most of the twentieth. This phenomenon, whilst particularly marked in Britain, has occurred over much of Europe as well, especially in those countries lying in the north-west parts of the continent. France, Belgium, the Netherlands, the Federal German Republic, Sweden, Denmark, Czechoslovakia, Switzerland and Italy have all recorded falling populations and there are indications that this decline in all probability extends beyond Europe eastwards into Asia. Such evidence would seem to suggest that there must be several common adverse factors to account for such a uniform decrease in the nightjar population.

## POPULATION IN GREAT BRITAIN

When the surveys for *The Atlas of Breeding Birds in Britain and Ireland* were carried out between 1968 and 1972 the editor, J. T. R. Sharrock, considered that a total population of some three thousand pairs of nightjars was a somewhat optimistic estimate. A further survey carried out in 1981 came to the conclusion that a figure of two thousand one hundred pairs was the maximum number that could reasonably be expected. All the indications would seem to point to the fact that there has been a further decline since then.

Precise reasons for this decline are uncertain, but one of the primary causes is likely to be a gradual change in climatic conditions. This, when combined with increased human pressure from agricultural expansion together with the widespread use of pesticides, may well have drastically reduced the insect populations on which the birds feed. To these factors may be added human recreational activi-

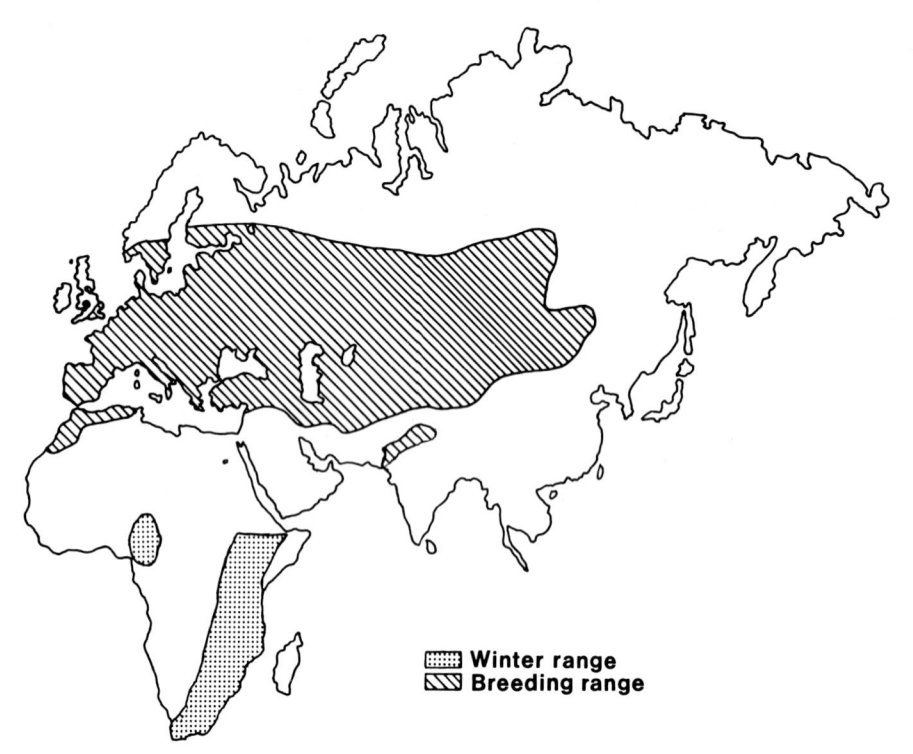

8. *Map of summer and winter distribution.*

ties such as walking, especially when accompanied by dogs, picnicking, horse riding and cross-country motor cycling, all of which cause severe disturbance to nesting and roosting birds during daylight hours. As the areas of available breeding habitat, especially heathland, decline so, correspondingly, the intensity of such activities increases the pressure on what remains.

With regard to the possible effect of climatic changes on the level of nightjar populations, there is good evidence to show that late cold spells in the spring, which have been a feature of many years since about 1960, particularly during May, have had a detrimental effect upon nightjar breeding success and hence on their population levels. Research undertaken in the early 1980s has shown that there is a reasonably close correlation between the date of the arrival of the male nightjars and the day on which the average minimum daily temperature reaches 10.5 C, and on that basis it was calculated that the average arrival date has been put back by approximately one week since the 1920s. Since the females arrive some ten to twelve days later than the males, it follows that the chances of rearing a successful second brood are considerably reduced.

HABITAT

The optimum habitat requirement for the European nightjar is an open well-drained site such as dry heathland or open newly planted conifer plantations. Occasionally birch, poplar or mixed woodland with oaks may be used. There appears to be some regional variation in habitat preference, for example in North Yorkshire forest sites are favoured rather than heath provided an open area of more than 2 hectares is available, since for the most part the nightjar takes its insect food above low vegetation, only very rarely hunting above the tree tops.

By contrast, in East Anglia heath with scattered birch seems to be preferred. The presence of trees in the vicinity of the nest is important as they are frequently used as song posts and lookouts.

Unusual nesting sites reported in Britain have included sand dunes, waste tips and, on very rare occasions, dense coppiced woodland; in the westernmost parts of the bird's range in Britain wet bog is sometimes used.

Observations in central Europe have indicated that the ability of the soil to absorb and later release heat is of considerable importance in the choice of suitable nest sites. In the USSR nightjars are absent from open plains and steppes, favouring forest fringes and wooded ravines as well as dry conifer forest and mixed woodland. In the Caucasus they are to be found foraging over fields and meadows up to the treeline at a height of around 2200 to 2500 metres.

Heathland, which is the most suitable breeding habitat for nightjars, has not only been under great pressure from reclamation schemes for agriculture but also from a process of natural degradation arising in part from changed agricultural practices. Sheep are now rarely pastured on heaths as they were formerly and the bracken is no longer cut and used for animal bedding. Since the advent of myxomatosis the decrease in the number of rabbits, whose browsing habits used also to keep the vegetation in check, has resulted in further encroachment of bracken, birch trees and so on which effectively destroy the heaths as suitable nightjar habitat.

Some indication of the loss of heathland is that since the 1880s the county of Dorset has lost 66 per cent of its heaths and the Breckland of East Anglia 88 per cent, much of it to forestry. A further difficulty is that, as the area of heaths become smaller, those that remain become more fragmented. An example of this trend has occurred in Dorset where, over the course of two centuries, eight main heath areas have been broken up into around one hundred smaller ones.

The decrease in nightjar numbers cannot be attributed solely to the reduction

9. *Open heathland as favoured by nightjars, with low vegetation and, particularly, with heather.*

10. *Male returning to the nest to relieve the sitting female. His wings are still raised as he waddles on his short legs towards the eggs.*

11. *Female returning to the nest in daylight; she moves very slowly and cautiously.*

12. *The female passing a solid ball of compacted insects to a young bird which is at the stage of being able to fly but is still dependent upon the adults for food.*

13. *A female nightjar feigning injury having been disturbed at the nest. While perched in this position she may rub her wings together to produce a rustling sound.*

in suitable heathland, however, since the bird is able to utilise forestry plantations in the early stages of their growth and also, for a while after they have been clear felled. This type of habitat has probably increased in parts of the nightjar's range in Britain, notably in East Anglia. There is as yet no clear explanation for this apparent anomaly.

## MIGRATION

Since it is both nocturnal and comparatively scarce the movements of the European nightjar are not very well understood once they leave their breeding areas, although they migrate across Europe on a broad front. Relatively small numbers of nightjars have been ringed in Britain (2001 up to the end of 1987 with only 56 recoveries) so little is known concerning the precise routes taken or the exact locations in which particular populations spend the winter. The primary wintering quarters of the European nightjar lie in sub-Saharan Africa as do those of the Asian populations which, apart from a few individuals who migrate to west Pakistan, also spend the winter in Africa. Once in Africa there is apparently no separation between the different subspecies. In their winter quarters the nightjars tend to avoid equatorial forests preferring the savannahs of eastern and southern Africa. A few are found in west Africa in the Gambia, Sierra Leone, Mauritania, Nigeria and Guinea Bissau but the numbers of birds wintering in the west of the continent are comparatively small when compared to those which fly on further south. R. E. Moreau and other observers have reported that nowhere does the European nightjar appear to be common and that, unlike some other winter visitors such as the swallow *Hirundo rustica*, the wintering nightjars do not outnumber the resident species.

14. Map indicating the probable migration routes of nightjars.

When breeding or in their winter quarters nightjars are not usually gregarious although on rare occasions as many as twelve may gather at a particularly rich feeding spot. Exceptionally, in May 1980, as many as 127 were counted within the space of ten minutes departing on migration in Africa from north-east Somalia, and a flock of fifty has been reported at Masirah island off the coast of Oman. In Arabia, through which many of the Asian subspecies pass, R. Meinertzhagen reported concentrations of immense numbers immediately prior to departure, but this account has never been corroborated by any other observers and the European nightjar would seem to be a scarce migrant through Saudi Arabia in the autumn. In spring the northward migration of the Asian subspecies appears to bypass the Middle East and reports of sightings from ships suggest that the birds may generally take an overwater route.

# Nesting and breeding behaviour

The nightjar is one of the latest of the summer breeding visitors to reach Britain and northern Europe. The males are the first to arrive at their breeding areas, usually around the end of the second week of May. The females follow about eleven days later although some may not appear until the second week of June. A few individual males may sometimes be found several days ahead of the main arrival at locations where they will not subsequently stay to breed, although in a number of cases these sites are known to have held breeding nightjars in the past. The date the birds arrive seems to vary little on average throughout their range in Britain and in much of western Europe.

## TERRITORIAL BEHAVIOUR

The territory in which the birds will nest is chosen by the male and once he has taken up residence he will patrol and defend it, strongly at first but with less intensity as the breeding season progresses. The size of the territory varies considerably according to the nature of the habitat. In a study undertaken in East Germany nests in heathland were found to be placed from 200 to 400 metres apart, whilst in East Anglia a comparable site produced a spacing ranging from 164 to 172 metres. In a pine forest in East Germany a density of 9.7 to 10.3 pairs of nightjars per square kilometre was found in the most suitable areas, with as many as 19.2 pairs per square kilometre in exceptional cases. The density of nests in given areas varies as the trees grow or the ground vegetation changes, which tends to limit the use of a particular site to no more than a few years at a time.

## DEFENSIVE BEHAVIOUR

The nightjar relies for safety on the extremely effective camouflage provided by its plumage which makes it almost invisible when on the ground. Although it may occasionally perch on a bough it will usually lie along it lengthways with head held low and eyes closed. The bird will remain immobile until an intruder is within a few metres before flying away, frequently giving an alarm call and wing-clapping as it goes. Should the male be disturbed at his roosting place he may 'churr' for a while and it is probable that the great majority of instances reported of daytime churring are the result of such occurrences. Sometimes when disturbed a nightjar will indulge in a distraction display including a form of injury feigning. This consists of a quite violent flapping flight whilst not flying far from the intruder; in this flight the wings may be bent back to form a W shape and the tail depressed. Alternatively the bird may fall to the ground where it may lie motionless for a short while. If this action fails to deter, the bird may return to land in front of the intruder, opening its mouth as wide as possible and at the same time making a hissing sound. On very rare occasions nightjars have been reported to have swooped at a human who has approached the nest too closely, behaviour similar to that employed by Arctic skuas and terns. When hunting away from the nest nightjars seem to be unafraid of man and will sometimes approach as close as 2 metres with no sign of concern.

## COURTSHIP

Much of the territorial advertisement by the male is by means of the prolonged churring song. Initially the 'churring' is produced for short periods but these become more frequent and prolonged after the females have arrived and courtship has commenced. The song is delivered from a number of perches around the territory, generally leafless twigs near the top of a tree, although other sites such as the roof of a cottage, a pole carrying power lines or the cable itself may be used. The male calls from a number of these song posts in turn, frequently wing-clapping (slapping the wings together above the body which produces a loud clapping sound) as he flies from one place to another and often giving the 'co-ic' call. Activity is greatest at dawn and, to a lesser extent, at dusk but is at a reduced level in cold or rainy conditions. The time at which nightjars become active at dusk varies according to the weather, the phase of the moon and the time of sunset. In East Germany, for instance, the birds become active from eleven minutes before sunset to twenty-six minutes after. In Suffolk it is usually more than thirty minutes after sunset, while in Finland, where there is little or no summer darkness, the birds have been heard to call as late as 3 am.

Apart from the use of song the males proclaim their territory by pursuing potential rivals in a chase involving wing-clapping interspersed with gliding flight in which the wings are held upwards in the form of a V, which emphasises the white wing bars. On rare occasions the defence of their territory may lead competing males to scuffle on the ground, pulling at each other's feathers; reports of fierce fights are uncommon.

Courtship display commences with the male flying slowly around the female in a butterfly-like manner interspersed with wing-clapping. This is usually followed by a gliding flight with wings raised above his back and the tail depressed and fanned out, clearly displaying the white wing bars and tail spots. Meanwhile the female may fly high and circle around before gliding down on rigid wings. Alternatively the male may lead the female downwards to the ground, wing-clapping as he goes. In a variation of this display the female lies on the ground with her wings and tail spread out whilst the male runs round her with fanned tail and drooping wings giving, at the same time, a quiet bubbling call. A similar murmuring note has been heard during the actual mating. Although copulation usually takes place on the ground it has also been observed to occur on one of the various song posts. Prior to copulation the male may partially open his wings whilst bobbing his body up and down and jerking his tail upwards and outwards, making the white spots at the tips of the outer tail feathers very prominent. Sometimes at this stage of his courtship the male will spring into the air and land on the back of the female. Display and mating may take place several times during the course of an evening.

## NEST SITE

Once the pair have mated they will start to search for a suitable place in the territory to lay the eggs, there being no nest as such. In this process of site selection the male plays the leading role, flying down to the spot on the ground which he has already chosen as a nest site, at the same time giving a muffled churring note in order to attract the attention of the female. He will then make a series of scraping movements with his feet whilst supporting himself on the carpal joints of his wings. At this stage of the breeding cycle the female follows the male constantly as he moves around his territory.

Nightjars begin to breed during the first summer after they have hatched and, should they survive for a second breeding season, there is some evidence to show that they exhibit a degree of fidelity to their original nest site. The nest itself is a bare scrape on the ground with no lining, frequently located close to a twig or stone which may be of use to the bird as a reference point when returning to the nest.

15. *Female perched on a bough — more often the bird would lie along the branch rather than across it.*

## ROOSTING

Until incubation starts the female generally roosts in a tree, but once she commences incubation she remains at the nest with the eggs and, later, the nestlings and does not go elsewhere to roost. The male prefers a bare patch of earth or a low tree stump, rarely higher than a metre above ground level, on which to roost, although sometimes he will lie along the bough of a tree. Exceptionally, nightjars have been seen to roost on pieces of cardboard or sacking. Usually the roost site is within 50 to a 100 metres of the nest but occasionally can be as far away as 200 metres. One nightjar to which a radio transmitter had been fitted was found to be roosting outside his own territory and in that of another male. If roosting on the ground in bright sunshine the male may move his body constantly around to face the sun so that he throws no obvious shadow and minimises heat absorption.

## INCUBATION

The two eggs are laid at night, the second from 24 to 36 hours after the first. The eggs are generally elliptical in shape with an average dimension of 31 by 22.5 mm and weigh approximately 8.2 grams. They have a greyish background colour flecked or marbled with yellowish brown or sepia. Clutches of three and four have been reported but these larger clutches are probably the result of two females laying in the same nest.

Incubation, which commences with the laying of the first egg, is undertaken by the female alone during daylight hours with the male taking his turn for short spells around dawn and dusk. When he returns to the nest from his roosting place at dusk he makes the 'co-ic' call and frequently indulges in wing-clapping while giving a bubbling call. The female replies from the nest and the male lands with his tail spread showing the white spots clearly. His return causes the female to make trembling movements with her wings and body and the male, in his turn, raises his wings high over his back before carefully lowering and folding them. Sometimes the female will fly off before the male lands on the nest.

## NESTLINGS

The eggs hatch after approximately

16. *Male nightjar hovering above a perched female.*

17. *Female with nestlings and broken eggshells. The cryptic coloration of the young makes them almost invisible at the right of the eggshells.*

nineteen days and the young nightjars emerge with their eyes open, being active straightaway. Strangely for a bird which is so dependent upon its cryptic coloration for safety, the empty shells are often left lying near the nest where they can easily be seen by any possible predator. For the first few nights the nestlings are brooded by the female and, until they are from sixteen to twenty days old, also during the day. The male takes his turn at dawn and dusk as he did during incubation. On taking over brooding the adult bird sways back and forth, an action which the young copy, and both adults and young bob their heads up and down. When the adult bird arrives back at the nest with food the nestlings beg with soft calls, head movements and flapping their wings and may even tug at the adult bird's rictal bristles.

The nestlings gain weight at approximately 4.5 grams per day for the first ten days, after which their weight stabilises at around 50 to 60 grams. When the young are becoming fledged, at around ten days, the adults pass the food to them in the form of a bolus (ball) of compacted insects about 30 mm in diameter. The actual transfer of the food takes about ten seconds. Whilst being fed the nestlings may alternate their behaviour, one gaping for food while the other crouches. After they have been fed the young back away from the nest for about a metre before defecating and as a result a ring of faeces forms around the nest site. If disturbed, the nestlings will crouch motionless and stretch themselves into an elongated posture, looking rather like cigars, or they may lie flat on the ground with outspread wings. From about the age of ten days they will often twist their necks and hiss or may even make a sudden upward leap, at the same time hissing and revealing the red linings to their mouths. This can be quite startling to an unwary intruder, especially since the nestlings are so well camouflaged that their presence may not have been suspected. The nestlings can just fly at about eighteen days but are dependent on their parents until they are around thirty days old.

## SECOND BROODS

The nightjar is partly double-brooded, although there is evidence to show that

19

far fewer second broods are being raised in Britain in the 1980s than was the case in the 1930s. The duration of the nightjars' stay in their breeding areas means that only those who arrive early are able to raise a second brood and this loss of breeding potential, because of climatic changes, has no doubt contributed to their population decrease over the years. Research has revealed that not all pairs who have sufficient time to raise a second brood actually do so, the number of pairs producing a second brood being only about 20 per cent. Another possible cause for the decrease in second broods is that lower average night temperatures may result in fewer night-flying insects being available, this loss of food affecting the ability to raise a second brood successfully. When there is a second brood the male takes over the care of the first brood from around the age of fourteen to sixteen days until they are independent; meanwhile the female tends the second brood, although the male will still relieve her for short periods around dawn and dusk.

Nightjars depart for Africa from about the second half of July, when the juveniles begin to leave. Most of the breeding sites have been vacated by the end of August and the majority of birds leave Britain during September. Remarkably, there is only one winter record of a nightjar, a bird found on the Isle of Mull in Scotland on 15th January 1974.

# Song

A number of birds such as the nightingale (*Luscinia megarhynchos*) and the bittern (*Botaurus stellaris*) are known mainly by sound rather than by sight. Similarly the low churring of the nightjar is its most widely recognised characteristic. Far more people are likely to have heard a nightjar while passing a quiet heath or a woodland edge on a summer's evening than ever see the bird itself. It is, therefore, mainly with a disembodied sound that most country dwellers and birdwatchers associate the nightjar. This strange rhythmic churring in the twilight adds to the mystery surrounding the bird and has helped to create many of the superstitions which have grown up around the nightjar over the centuries. It would be wrong, however, to imagine that the 'churring' call is the only sound made by the nightjar: its vocalisations are quite extensive although not all of them could be considered musical and some are as yet not fully understood.

The long churring note which is the best known advertising call of the nightjar has been described as a 'sustained vibrant churring trill, though low pitched'. Once heard it is distinctive, but in some circumstances it is necessary for the listener to be aware of the similarity of the sound to the stridulation of the mole-cricket (*Gryllotalpa gryllotalpa*), although the call of this cricket is at a higher frequency than that of the nightjar. This large insect is comparatively

18. *The huge size of the nightjar's mouth is very well shown as the bird yawns.*

rare in Britain, being for the most part confined to that part of the country south of the Thames with its main area in the Wiltshire Avon valley. Another source of confusion, especially for the inexperienced observer, exists in the New Forest area where the wood cricket (*Nembobius sylvestris*) makes a rather similar sound. There is also the possibility of being misled by the call of the natterjack toad (*Bufo calamita*), but again the difficulty arises mainly for those who have never heard a nightjar call before. In southern Europe there is a similar problem with the song of the vineyard mole-cricket (*Gryllotalpa vineae*).

The churring song can continue uninterrupted for as long as nine minutes and there are reports of prolonged singing (with only very short pauses) of up to 19½ minutes. The sound is produced at a speed of 28 to 42 notes per second. When the bird begins to call at dusk the duration of the song is generally shorter compared with later in the evening. The churring song appears to rise and fall, a phenomenon believed at one time to be caused by the singing bird moving its head from side to side but now thought to relate to the bird's breathing rhythm. Quite frequently at the end of a spell of churring the sounds fall away rather like a clockwork toy running down. Some observers have stated that the female occasionally gives the churring call, but if this is so it would appear to be an uncommon event and the song to be only about twenty seconds in length. The churring call is heard immediately following the arrival of the male bird in May and continues with decreasing frequency, particularly after the third week of July, until late August.

The nightjar also often uses a call which may be fairly represented as 'co-ic'. This call, sharp and penetrating, is usually uttered whilst the nightjar is in flight but is occasionally given immediately prior to the bird taking flight. Again, in the majority of cases it is the male who calls but the female does so occasionally. The 'co-ic' call is frequently given by nightjars whilst in their winter quarters but the churring call is very rarely heard, although there have been reports of it from Pilanesberg in South Africa and elsewhere.

Should a nightjar become very anxious, such as when an intruder approaches its nest, it may give a 'chenk' call somewhat similar to the alarm call of the blackbird, which is often heard in a garden. The nightjar's alarm call is of low intensity, however, and does not carry for more than a few metres. While feeding and brooding both adults have been heard to make a low puffing sound, 'wuff-wuff-wuff', which acts as a contact call but may also at times alert the nestlings to dangers.

This is only a brief outline of the vocalisations of which the nightjar is capable, but many of the slight variations of sound are difficult to express in words. There are, however, a number of recordings available which provide a valuable guide to the calls discussed.

### WING-CLAPPING

Wing-clapping conveys a message and is an integral part of the sound communication of the nightjar, albeit a mechanical one. The sound is created by the wings striking together over the bird's back and sometimes by slapping them together at the end of the down beat. Twenty-five wing claps in succession have been counted, but generally no more than five or six are heard. When the bird is disturbed at the nest it may wing-clap as it flies away and also give a call which could be rendered as 'oak-oak'.

# Food

The nightjar is an entirely insectivorous bird and virtually all its food is taken whilst in flight. It is superbly adapted for this, its long wings and tail enabling it either to twist and turn with great agility or, more rarely, to hover momentarily when in pursuit of its prey. Moths (Lepidoptera) of many species make up the bulk of its food, followed by beetles (Coleoptera) and true flies (Diptera), whilst a small proportion of its diet consists of a variety of insect families including craneflies (Tipulidae) and ants (Formicidae). The precise composition of the diet varies considerably depending on the season and on the insect food available at the time, which can be greatly affected by temperature and weather conditions. Figures produced in a survey undertaken in East Germany showed that adult nightjars took approximately 62.4 per cent of Lepidoptera, 12.2 per cent Diptera, 7.7 per cent Coleoptera, 7.2 per cent Trichoptera, 5.7 per cent Neuroptera and 4.8 per cent unspecified insects.

The feeding strategy of the nightjar is one of aerial pursuit, usually at low levels and only rarely above the treetops. The prey is generally approached from below or sometimes from the side. When feeding low above heather or bracken the nightjar flies with its normal flapping flight alternating with glides in which the wings are held above the back in a V shape. Quite often a nightjar has been seen to feed in a similar way to that employed by the flycatchers (Muscicapidae) by making short sallies from a perch, taking prey and then returning to the same perch. This frequently occurs after the main period of feeding activity at dusk. Despite a belief to the contrary nightjars do not trawl for food by flying with their huge mouths open, although in view of the disproportionate size of the mouth in comparison with the rest of the body it is not difficult to see how this particular absurdity has arisen. It has been found that nightjars invariably open their bills only immediately prior to taking their prey. It has been reported that nightjars sometimes feed on the ground, which appears to be confirmed by the discovery in their crops of the remains of flightless worker ants and, on one occasion, of a flightless female glowworm. Nevertheless this seems to be an unusual form of feeding.

Many nightjars captured for ringing have been found with abdominal bulges as a result of their gizzards being crammed with insects. Since the avian gizzard is not normally used for the storage of food this may, perhaps, be an adaptation peculiar to the nightjar. It would enable the bird to take as many insect prey as possible at the times when insects are most abundant, such as early in the evening. Radio tracking of marked birds and intensive observations have shown that in their excursions for food during the first two hours of their evening activities, nightjars may feed over deciduous woodland and farmland as far as 6 kilometres away from the breeding site.

## NESTLING FOOD

As might be expected, when newly hatched the young are fed the more delicate Microlepidoptera and Diptera, which means the adults must hunt very low over the ground, rather like the swallows. Once the nestlings have reached the age of about ten days their food is more or less the same as that of the adults. In a research programme undertaken in East Germany to determine precisely what insect prey the adult birds bring to their nestlings, neck collars placed on a number of nightjar nestlings to prevent them swallowing the bolus (a ball of compacted insects about 30 mm in diameter) brought to them by the adult birds. These food balls were then analysed both quantitatively and qualitatively in order to identify their contents. The size of the food items in the bolus given to the nestlings from two to four days old was 7.9 to 10.2 mm, but for the older nestlings from five to seventeen days, the size of the prey rose from 11.2 to 13.9 mm. As the young developed the percentage of small items such as Diptera dropped from 31 to 14 per cent, whilst other larger Lepidoptera increased from 24.3 to 45.5 per cent during the same period.

## DRINK

Nightjars have occasionally been observed drinking in flight in much the same manner as the swallow, that is, by flying very low and dipping their bills into the water in order to scoop up the liquid. However, it would seem likely that the birds obtain most of their liquid requirements from their prey.

# Folklore

Being mainly nocturnal or at best crepuscular, the nightjar is rarely seen by the casual observer. Add to this its strange, almost disembodied, song and over the course of the centuries a considerable body of folklore is bound to develop. When glimpsed at dusk or at night its silent twisting flight did nothing to dispel the illusion that the bird was a ghostly spirit of the night. Since man basically lives a daylight existence and has always had an instinctive and deep-rooted fear of night creatures, it is easy to understand how he would equate the nightjar with dark thoughts of death and witchcraft.

In much the same way that owls have sadly and quite unjustly been singled out as victims of such superstitions, so to a somewhat lesser degree has the nightjar. A good illustration is given by Gilbert White in whose parish of Selborne in Hampshire, where he was perpetual curate for much of the second half of the eighteenth century, nightjars were relatively common. Gilbert White reported the widespread belief that nightjars, or 'fern owls' as he often referred to them, did great harm to young calves by striking at them with their beaks and infecting them with a malady which he called 'Puckeridge' and which caused the animals a great deal of pain and distress. This infection was caused by the warble fly (*Hypoderma bovis*) which lays its eggs under the skin on the animal's back, particularly on the rump and along the spine. When the eggs hatched the resulting maggots burrowed their way out through the hide of the animal leaving the infection behind. Apart from the damage done to the health of the cattle, the holes left behind quite ruined the value of the hide after slaughter. So deep rooted was the belief that this malady was the work of the nightjar that many country people in Hampshire and Sussex called the nightjar itself 'Puckeridge'. Gilbert White himself was well aware that this particular belief was pure invention. He had observed the bird very closely and even analysed the stomach contents of specimens he had shot and was completely sure that they ate nothing but insects. He also recognised the fact that their bills were far too weak to penetrate the hide of a cow. Gilbert White proceeds to describe how unfairly 'this harmless ill fated bird falls under a double imputation which it by no means deserves'.

The belief that nightjars sucked the milk of cows and goats, first reported by Aristotle, was widespread throughout Europe; the German name *Ziegenmelker*, the Spanish *chotocabras gris* and the Russian *kozodoi* all refer to this supposed activity. The myth that nightjars steal milk from domestic livestock probably arose because animals feeding on heathland might very well have attracted insects which in turn were preyed upon by the nightjars. Under such circumstances a goatherd or cowman seeing the nightjars flying around his flock and then noticing that the teats of one of his animals were leaking milk, a not unusual occurrence if it had not been milked for some time, might easily have assumed that the nightjar was responsible. The Greek writer, Dion, about AD 200, suggested that nightjars could be captured by doctoring the teats of goats. In some countries it was believed that not only did the nightjar steal the milk but that, as a result of this activity, the teat itself would wither away and the animal would become blind. Pliny believed that nightjars themselves were blind in the daytime and only regained their sight after dark.

Many of the popular folk names for the nightjar such as 'goatsucker', 'goat owl' and 'goat chaffer' refer to its supposed milk stealing activities. Other names such as 'night churr', 'scissor grinder', 'churr owl', 'eve churr' and 'jar owl' refer to its song. The similarity of its churring to the sound of a spinning wheel gave rise to such names as 'wheelbird', 'spinner' and the Welsh name of *aderyn-y-droell* which means spinning-wheel bird. Some names refer to its diet of insects and examples of these are 'moth hawk', 'nighthawk', 'night swallow' (in German, *Nachtschwalbe*) or 'dor hawk', dor being an old name for beetle.

The people of Nidderdale in North Yorkshire once believed the nightjar to be the repository for the souls of unbaptised children condemned to wander about the world for ever. They referred to the nightjars as 'gabble ratchets', another word for corpse hounds, a variant of 'Gabriel's hounds' which, it was said, could be heard baying in the night air. Since it is difficult to equate the call of the nightjar with that of a baying hound such appellations as these and 'devil hounds' would appear to have been more appropriately applied to the owls. In Shropshire the nightjar was sometimes referred to as 'lichfowl', again meaning a corpse-fowl, and in parts of Germany the name *Todtenvogel*, meaning death bird, was sometimes used.

It is sad that such an inoffensive bird should have gained a sinister reputation and have been so maligned throughout the ages, a bird whose only sin appeared to be that, as Gilbert White said, 'it was simply a bird of the night.'

# Useful information

FURTHER READING
Berry, R., and Bibby, C. J. 'A Breeding Study of Nightjars', *British Birds*, 74 (1981), 161-9.
Cramp, S. (chief editor). *The Birds of the Western Palaearctic*, volume 4. Oxford University Press, 1985, pages 620-36.
Cresswell, B. H. *The Nightjar Project: Some Results of the Radio Tracking Work.* Stour Ringing Group Report, 1985, page 52.
Cresswell, B. H. *Nightjars: A Preview of Some Early Results from Analysis of 1986 Data.* Stour Ringing Group Report, 1986, page 31.
Lack, D. L. 'Some Breeding Habits of the European Nightjar', *Ibis*, 1932, pages 266-84.
Swainson, C. *Provincial Names and Folklore of British Birds*, 1885.

RECORDINGS
Lewis, V. *The Cassette Album of British Bird Vocabulary*, volume 5.
Palmer, S., and Boswall, J. *A Field Guide to the Bird Songs of Britain and Europe*, cassette 6A.
Roche, J. C. *The Bird Walker: A Dictionary of Bird Songs from Britain, Europe and North Africa*, cassette 1.

ACKNOWLEDGEMENTS
Illustrations are acknowledged as follows: Frank V. Blackburn, cover, 2, 10, 11, 12, 13, 15; Silvestris, courtesy of the Frank Lane Picture Agency, 7; Michael Gore, 6; Eric and David Hosking, 3, 5, 16, 17, 18; Alan Parker, 4. All other illustrations are by the author.